DAVID TAYLOR'S
MIGHTY ANIMALS

A round-the-world journey of adventure

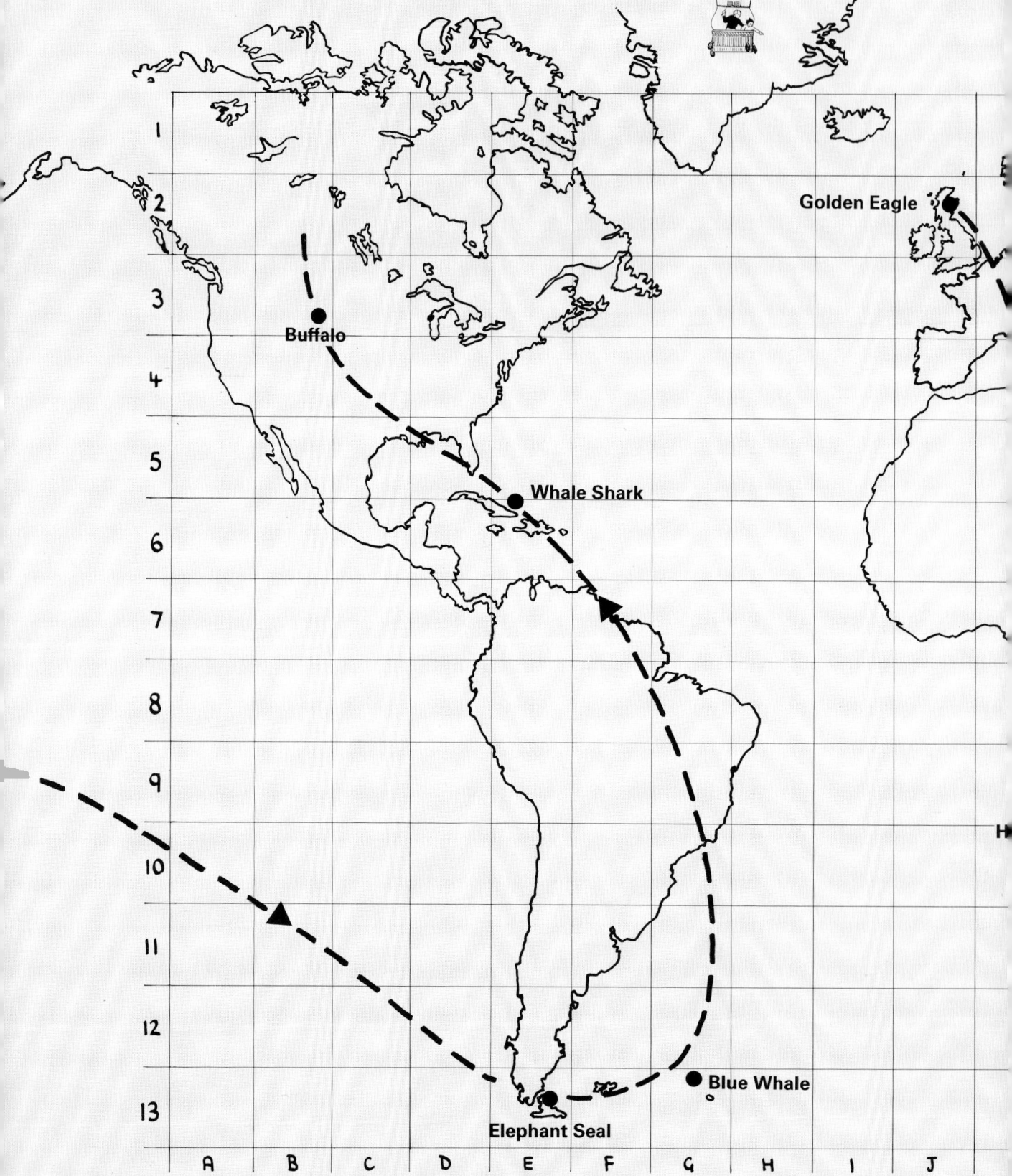

1

2 **Golden Eagle** ●

3
● **Buffalo**

4

5
● **Whale Shark**

6

7

8

9

10

11

12

● **Blue Whale**

13

Elephant Seal

A B C D E F G H I J

DAVID TAYLOR'S
MIGHTY ANIMALS

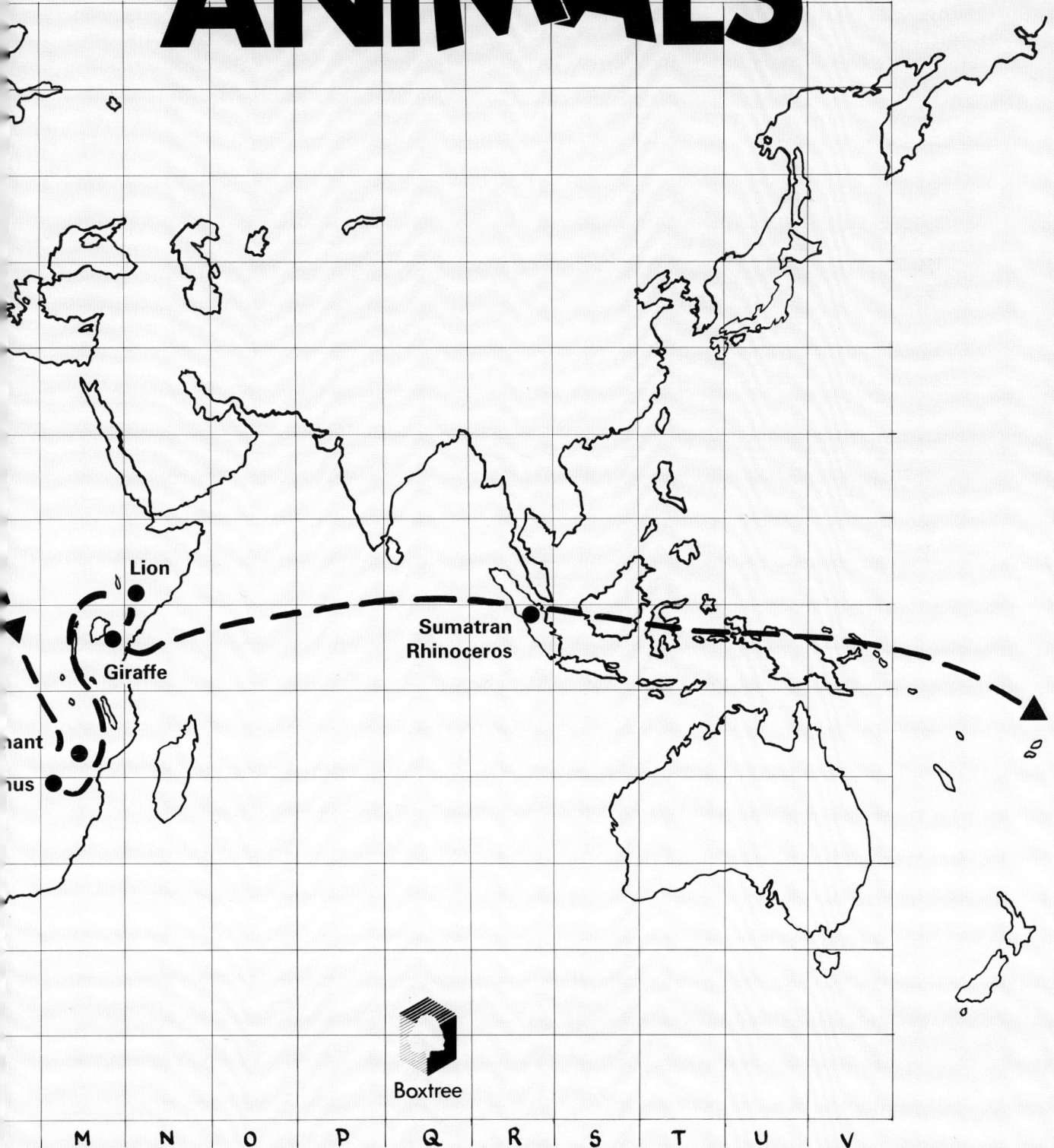

Lion

Giraffe

hant

hus

Sumatran
Rhinoceros

Boxtree

M   N   O   P   Q   R   S   T   U   V

INTRODUCTION

All animals are experts at what they do. Some are tough survivors who have learned how to live in what are to us forbidding environments of temperature extremes, aridity or great pressure. They have developed the ability to struggle unceasingly for scarce food supplies or to cope with unrelenting competition and predatory enemies. Some, like the dragonfly or lynx, are skilled warriors, some, like insects which size for size demonstrate more muscle power than elephants, are surprisingly strong. So how do I define MIGHTY in relation to animals?

I believe certain creatures, by their *combination* of size, strength and lifestyle deserve the description. Awesome to watch in action, formidable when roused to attack or defend (and by no means all of them are carnivorous hunters), they powerfully impress puny, physically rather unaccomplished, primates like me (and you).

From a wider range of creatures which I think would qualify as 'mighty', I have selected ten. They live in many different parts of the world and although you may well know something about them, I can guarantee there is much you have yet to discover. To this end I have recently been building a marvellous hot air balloon. Its basket or gondola will hold two persons, you and me. There is space for gas bottles to heat the burner that fills the balloon's canopy with lighter, hot air, for food supplies, sleeping bags and other necessary equipment. My idea is for us to sail off through the skies on a voyage of exploration, riding the wind to the four corners of the earth so that we can visit my ten mighty beasts.

If you are game (no need to worry about air sickness – I have some special tablets), grab your camera and notebook, your binoculars and tape recorder, and we'll get on our way. First stop . . . well, let's wait and see! Up and away.

Acknowledgements

The publishers would like to thank the following for permission to reproduce photographs in this book:

Bruce Coleman Limited: pages 8, top left (Jane Burton); page 8, bottom right (Jeff Foott); page 9 (Jeff Foott); page 12 (Gerald Cubitt); page 13, left, (Norman Myers); page 13, right (Dieter and Mary Plage); page 14 (Rod Williams); page 16 (Michael Freeman); page 17 (Simon Trevor); page 19 (Gunter Ziesler); page 20 (Simon Trevor); page 21 (Len Rue Junior); page 22 (Masood Quarishy); page 24 (Gunter Ziesler); page 25 (Carol Hughes); page 26 (Masood Quarishy); page 28 (Alain Compost); page 29 (Gerald Cubitt); page 30 (F. Vollmar); page 32 (Frans Lanting); page 34 (Gunter Ziesler); page 35 (WWF/AI Giddings); page 38 (Jeff Foott); page 43 (Mark Boulton); page 44 (John M Burnley); page 45 (Jeff Foott). Heather Angel: page 37.
Oxford Scientific Films: page 41 (Pam and Willy Kemp).

First published in Great Britain in 1990
by Boxtree Limited
Text copyright © David Taylor 1990
Artwork copyright © Boxtree Limited 1990
Front cover illustration and all artwork by David Quinn
Designed by Groom and Pickerill

Typeset by York House Typographic
Origination by Culver Graphics
Printed in Singapore
For Boxtree Limited,
36 Tavistock Street,
London WC2E 7PB

British Library Cataloguing in Publication Data
Taylor, David, *1934–*
Mighty animals.
1. Large animals.
I. Title II. Quinn, David
591
ISBN 1-85283-035-2

CONTENTS

Abbreviations

mm	millimetre
cm	centimetre
m	metre
km	kilometre
kmh	kilometres per hour
ha	hectare
gm	gram
kg	kilogram

Below, gleaming gently in the early morning sun, the twin conical towers of a castle. We wave to a red-haired man who stands on the turreted ramparts gazing up at us as we drift by. The castle is perched on the edge of a broad expanse of gleaming black water beyond which gentle purple-tinged slopes press close to a range of mountains still smeared with snow. Although the mountainsides are, for the most part, heather-clad shoulders with fields of dark scree and eruptions of granite boulders, there is one place, a kilometre or so wide, where, aeons ago, the mountainside broke away to leave the high sheer cliffs of grey stone that our balloon is now approaching.

'Where are we, David?' you ask. I trim the burners and then look back at the castle.

'The fiery headed gentleman is, I believe, the owner of all the land we can see, but he *doesn't* own the magnificent

Emblem of a Roman legion – the proud eagle.

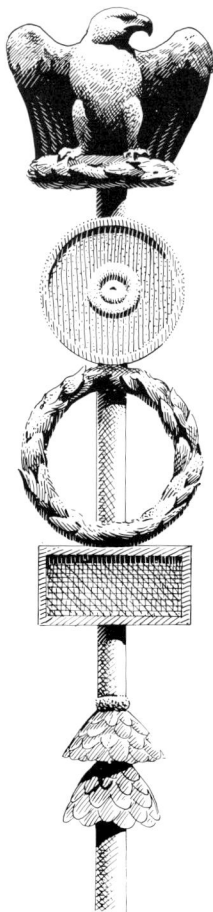

creatures we have travelled here to see.'

The balloon is now hanging almost motionless a few metres from the cliff face. It's tricky to hold it here. Pointing towards a rocky ledge where a jumble of dead twigs is lying, I'm about to explain when a shadow darkens the sky above us. There is a rush of wind, a short screech and two yellow claws snatch at my hair. Both of us tumble down in the basket as powerful dark wings beat overhead. The balloon starts to descend, yawing drunkenly. The shadow vanishes, the wind catches us and with relief I see the cliff's face begin to recede.

Above us, the sharp and gleaming eyes of the *golden eagle*, standing on the ledge with its chick in the eyrie (nest) beside it, glare at us and our curious craft.

The sun-bird

We are in the mountains of the north of Scotland. All of Britain's remaining and endangered golden eagles, with the exception of one pair that are now nesting in the Lake District of England, live in the Scottish hill country. Like some other birds of prey, they have suffered from persecution by egg collectors, the poisons and guns of gamekeepers and farmers, the increased use of pesticides in agriculture and the relentless spread of 'civilisation' into the once peaceful, wilder corners of the land.

From the earliest times, the eagle was venerated, feared and admired in almost every country where it existed. It was honoured in the ancient myths of Egypt, Persia, Assyria and India, and considered to be the associate of the great god Zeus of the Greeks. The Roman legions carried standards bearing the emblem of the eagle and when a Roman emperor died an eagle was let fly from his funeral pyre. Later the eagle took its place in the coat of arms of the Emperor Constantine, Queen Mary of England, of the states of Austria, Russia, Poland ('the Land of the White Eagle'), France and the United States – truly a noble bird. It was considered king of the heavens, the bringer of storms and

The golden eagle does not take kindly to visitors to its nest.

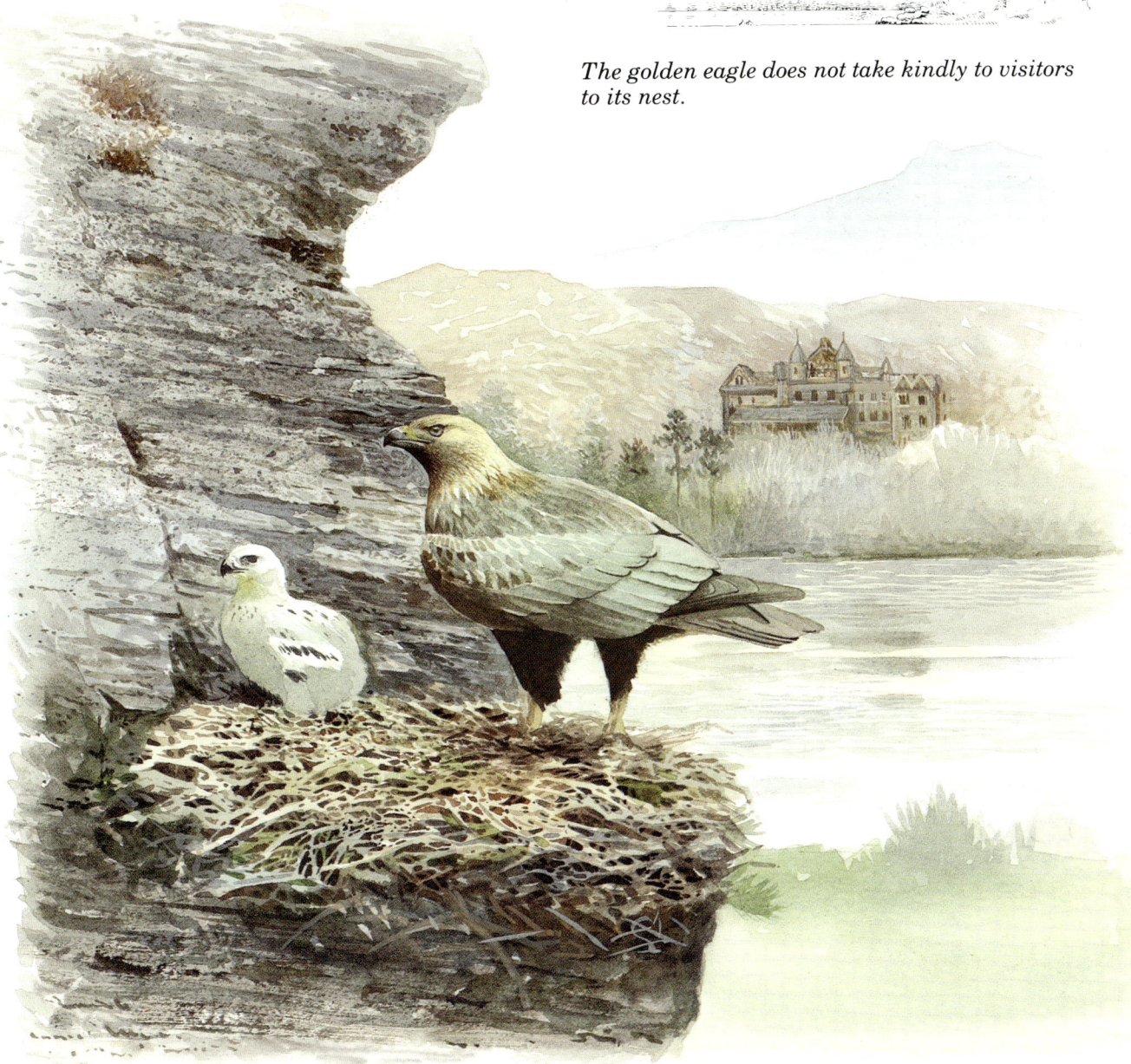

thunderbolts, the sun-bird who could stare into the sun's light without being dazzled. Many believed it never grew old because it was able, periodically, to renew its youth. It would first fly so near the sun that its feathers burst into flames, and then dive into the sea to quench the fire. Returning to its nest, it would patiently wait for the new plumage to grow, and with it, new youth.

The golden eagle is one of the best-known eagles and outside Scotland is also to be found in mountainous regions of continental Europe, Asia and North America. A pair of eagles build a huge nest (eyrie) of sticks on cliffs or tall trees,

returning year after year to lay a clutch of 1-4 white eggs mottled with brown. The young are covered in white down which is replaced by dark brown juvenile plumage at about ten weeks of age. They moult annually until the wonderful golden brown colour of the adult is acquired at four years of age. The Tatar people of what is now Soviet Asia still hunt deer and wolves using golden eagles, and in Europe, in the days of medieval falconry, they were flown only by kings.

Lords of the air

Eagles, who hunt prey by day, are widely distributed around the world. There are

The golden eagle is the noblest of all hunting birds.

30 species of *booted* (with legs feathered to the toes) *eagle* in a family that includes the golden eagle, 11 species of *fish eagle*, including the endangered *white-tailed sea eagle* (now being reintroduced into the north of Scotland) and the famous *bald eagle* of the USA, 12 species of *snake-eating eagle* including the *bateleur* (juggler) *eagle* so named because of its aerial acrobatic skills during courtship, and several others such as the mighty *harpy eagle* of South America and the very rare, strange-faced, *monkey-eating eagle* of the Philippines, of which perhaps only a dozen or two still survive.

Although the golden eagle is an impressively big bird, with the heavier female weighing 6-7 kg and sporting a wingspan of up to 2.5 m, it isn't as heavy as the harpy eagle which sometimes reaches over 9 kg. Harpy eagles, however, need to

hunt among trees, and so they have shorter (2.25 m), broader wings. The biggest wingspan among eagles is displayed by the *wedge-tailed eagle*, with some females claimed to have measured 3 m from tip to tip.

Could such great birds carry off human babies, as is so often alleged in old legends and fables? Experts think not. An 8 lb (3.63 kg) baby is probably too much for any living species of eagle, but ... *Steller's sea eagle* can lift seal pups, young Arctic foxes and large fish from sea or ground, harpy eagles can snatch up mammals such as monkeys, coati-mundis and opossums, a golden eagle has been seen to fly up with an adult fox (probably weighing something between 5 and 6 kg) in its talons, and American bald eagles are known to have carried off lambs and deer fawns.

The famous American bald eagle takes a meal of fish.

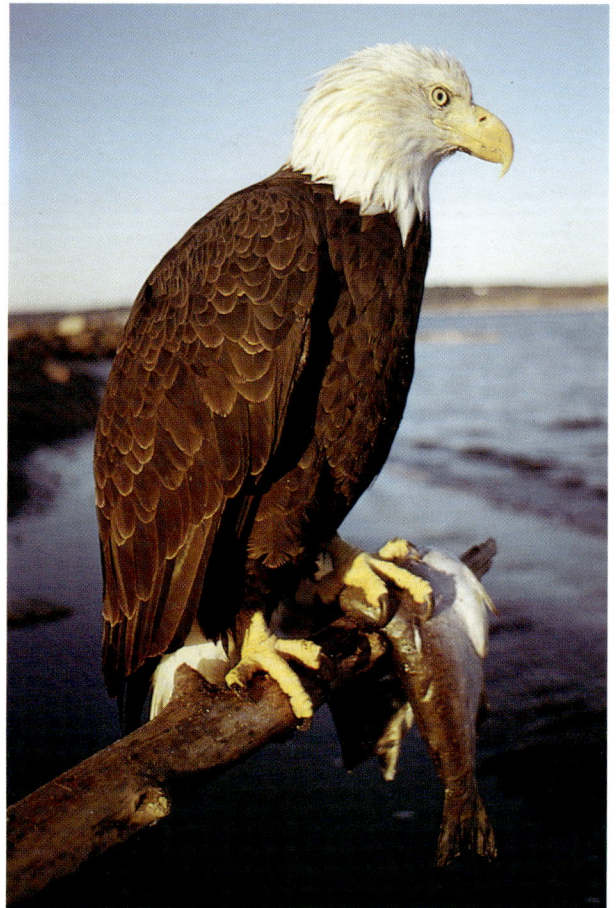

An American golden eagle feeds on a jack rabbit.

Eagles may not be stealers of infants, but they are expert at many other things. They can fly far and high; *steppe eagles* have been found at a height of 7,925 m on Mount Everest. Like all birds of prey, they have incredibly acute vision that is about three times sharper than yours and mine. Golden eagles are said to be able to spot a rabbit at a distance of 3 km and other species can pick out a grasshopper sitting motionless almost 300 m away. Like other birds, they can see in colour, but they cannot smell. (Some birds, such as the New World vultures, kiwis and petrels, are able to smell things.)

* * * * *

'Why do people deliberately kill eagles?' you ask as we move away.

'Well, often it's because of sheep farming. Eagles will feed on dead sheep that they come across, and sometimes take live lambs. They rarely do much damage to flocks, but sheep farmers don't like losing even a single lamb. Eagles are nowadays protected in most countries, but illegal killing still goes on. And many die of pesticide poisoning. Like other birds of prey, they eat animals which carry the poisons in their bodies after eating seeds, fruits and vegetables sprayed with chemicals used in agriculture to control pests. These poisons build up in the eagles' bodies. Some, like DDT, make the shells of eggs laid by the birds too thin – so they break and kill the developing chick. Other pesticides, the more modern ones, attack various organs of the bird's body, producing illness and then death.'

'Same old story,' I hear you mutter. 'Why can't we leave animals alone?'

The eagle watches intently from afar as we begin to soar up into his realm.

9

C rack! crack! crack! The sound of fire crackers far below breaks the quiet of the sun-drenched morning. The basket rocks slightly and a splinter of wood comes spinning up to land in your hair.

Crack! We both go to the sides and peer over. Three hundred metres below, the savannah plain, paling to yellow in the late summer heat and dotted with untidy clumps of grey-green scrub, runs in all directions to the horizon.

There is another, even louder crack. Then I catch sight of them, three figures standing beside a grey-black mound. They are looking up and one is pointing a stick . . . not a stick! And the mound . . . I recognise the outline.

A modern tragedy – poachers steal an elephant's rightful property.

'Get down!' I yell and yank at the controls. The burners open their throats and the blue flames roar upward. We must gain height quickly. 'Get on the radio and call up the police on channel 9,' I throw the hand-microphone across to you. 'Tell them we've run into some poachers who don't like us interfering with their dirty business, and give them a map reference.'

Crack! This time I actually hear the bullet hum as it travels past the basket. But we are already rising rapidly.

Half an hour later, after making sure through our binoculars that the coast is now clear, the poachers having fled with their booty, we land and walk over to the grey mound we had seen from the sky. It is indeed the sad remains of one of our mighty animals. Bloody, jagged-edged craters yawn where the tusks have been hacked out of its head. Another *elephant*

has been brutally struck off the list of Africa's fast-shrinking herds.

Giants of yesterday and today

The elephant must surely be the mightiest land animal alive. Measuring up to 4 m high at the shoulder and weighing as much as 6½ tonnes, Jumbo is a magnificent creature. Long ago there were over 350 kinds of elephant in the world. Perhaps the most famous of these extinct forms was the *mammoth*. It was about as big as a modern *Indian* elephant with a high, pointed skull and unique, spiralling tusks whose tips pointed towards one another. The tusks were 3 to 4 m long and would each weigh over 100 kg, longer and heavier than those of the biggest living *African* elephant, but not as huge as the 5 m tusks that were carried by another long-gone elephant, the *Straight-tusked elephant* which inhabited northern Germany about two million years ago.

Mammoths lived in the Pleistocene epoch, 50,000 to one million years ago. They were adapted to a cold, Arctic climate, being covered with long yellow-brown, woolly hair that almost reached the ground, and with patches of thicker black hairs on the cheeks, flanks and abdomen. They had small furry ears and a short tail tipped with a tuft of long stiff bristles. During periods of warm weather, they migrated north to follow the ice fields, grazing on grasses, sedges, and other plants such as wild thyme, Alpine poppy and crowfoot.

There are two reasons why we know so much about the mammoths. Firstly, early man, who hunted them, left marvellous cave paintings of them. Secondly, and more dramatically, scientists have found the deep-frozen bodies of mammoths in the permanently icy soil of the Siberian tundra. Many are so well preserved that they look as if they died only yesterday, with fresh plant food still green and succulent in their stomachs. Most exciting of all is the possibility that one day in the future mammoths may live again! Scientists who specialise in genetic engineering are capable of extracting genetic chemicals, which still carry the hereditary 'blueprint' of complete mammoths, from preserved mammoth body cells, and could use these when fertilising an ordinary female elephant by artificial means. Imagine – 21-23 months later (the elephant pregnancy period is the longest of any mammal) – the modern world's first mammoth baby could be born – 1,000 centuries after its parents grazed the Siberian land!

The woolly mammoth – could it be re-created in the future?

Other extinct elephants include the *Mastodon*, an inhabitant of all continents except Australia. Many fossil *Mastodons* have been dug up in the USA and Canada. These animals, longer and lower than modern elephants, fed on leaves in the wet, lush ice-age forests. There was also the mini-elephant, a dwarf form found in the Mediterranean regions, the smallest being a 1 m high variety from Crete, and the biggest elephant so far discovered (in Kent), a giant that stood almost 5 m high. (A mini-elephant would have made a good pet!)

Replaceable teeth

As we turn away from the body of the poachers' victim, we notice that a small group of elephants has emerged from a

The leader of an elephant family is usually an old female.

stand of acacia trees some 500 m away. A big female, leader of the herd, is looking in our direction, her ears flapped forwards to act as receiving dishes to collect more sound and her sensitive trunk held up, S-shaped, to sniff the air for information about us. (Elephants are very short-sighted.) We can tell immediately, because of the big ears, that these are African elephants; the ears of Asiatic or Indian elephants are much smaller.

Elephants are members of a group of mammals called Proboscidea (animals with a proboscis – a long snout). Surprisingly, their closest *living* relative is the *hyrax*, a small furry animal, rather like a large guinea-pig, which lives in Africa and parts of Arabia.

Although elephants are vegetarians, they are not ruminants which chew the cud, and don't possess four stomachs like cows, buffalo or antelopes. They have a simple single stomach and digest their food mainly in the large intestine, rather like horses. To grind the tough branches,

leaves and fibrous plants which they eat, they have enormous teeth, each one about as big as a house brick and weighing 2 to 5 kg. Only four teeth are in use at any one time. As the two teeth at the front wear down, they fall out and are replaced by two new ones moving forwards from the back of the mouth. Throughout its life an elephant can call on a total of 24 teeth; after they are all used up, an elephant in the wild will starve to death. Nevertheless elephants, both in the wild and in zoos, can reach an age of 70 years and perhaps more.

On the rampage

Elephants are intelligent animals and also have a good memory. Elephant friends that I only see once every year or two instantly recognise me and make a fuss, tickling me with their trunk tips, purring like enormous cats and even squeaking with delight.

Even so, they can be dangerous too, as lions, tigers – and humans, know to their cost. Male elephants are particularly tricky when they are in the curious state called 'musth'. This is a physiological phe-

12

nomenon, not well understood, that occurs usually once a year and can last for a few days or a few months. The bulls become restless and aggressive and secrete an oily liquid from glands on their temples. And of course elephants never like being harassed, threatened or teased.

The African elephant has big ears which it flaps forward when it charges.

Once in a while elephants get roaring drunk after eating overripe fruit, particularly that of the so-called Miracle tree. When they detect the rather boozy smell of the berries on the wind, they'll travel miles to hold a rather alcoholic feast. And I've had to treat tipsy elephants who stole overripe medlar fruit when I was travelling with them across Spain. Not an easy job. In 1974 a herd of about 150 drunken elephants who had imbibed illegal alcoholic liquor made by villagers in West Bengal went on the rampage, killing five persons and injuring a dozen more. All in all between 200 and 500 people are killed each year by wild elephants, the majority of them in Africa, and occasionally elephants in zoos attack their keepers.

A shrinking population

It is a sad fact that elephants themselves are under threat nowadays. Poachers still kill them, just to take their tusks which are then sold for fashioning into ivory ornaments and trinkets. Poaching alone has reduced the African elephant population by more than HALF during the 1980's, from 1.2 million to less than 600,000. About 100,000 African elephants are slaughtered by poachers every year!

Then there's the ever-diminishing elephant habitat. Men, with their agriculture and their development of land, have so reduced the space needed by elephants that they no longer find a welcome in their old haunts. With fewer trees to crop, less space to roam, elephants do more damage to the available vegetation. The result is that in some places they must survive with very little tree cover, and the unshaded African sun on their backs produces changes in their blood vessels that can lead to an early death.

This baby Indian elephant is only one day old.

RIVERBED BALLET DANCER

You are grumbling again. Despite what I consider to have been a perfect landing right on target, it is obvious you don't like *mud*.

'Of all places!' you repeat. 'A mud bank slap in the middle of a river.' Brushing off another cluster of flies, I walk round the basket and begin to pull in the shroud that is our deflated balloon.

'But I'm *exactly* where I plan to be,' I say. 'This is *it*! What's a little mud between friends?' Wordless, you shake a leg, caked in sticky brown mud, towards me.

'Ah. But think of the animals I have brought you to see.'

You look around at the broad, black river, the banks covered in tall grass, dark green bushes beyond. A white stork stands contemplating the water at the river's edge with total concentration. A pair of black vultures lazily ride a thermal above our heads. The evening sky is a vast canvas of some modern painter slashed with broad strokes of flamingo-pink, orange and pearl.

'Crocodile!' you cry. 'Sacred in ancient times – killer of horses and men – a mighty river animal. That's it!'

'Wrong!'

'What then? Surely this river is in Africa – or have we landed in the Americas, in which case it must be an alligator?'

'Africa yes. Alligators no. As I said, we've landed exactly where I planned – right on top of a mud bank which is the nursery for the young of one of Africa's most impressive animals – and, moreover, an underwater ballet dancer.' No wonder you look puzzled.

'Come on, put on your wetsuit – we'll take a dip in the river and see if I can introduce you to it.'

Still puzzled, you change into your scuba gear and I do likewise. Fortunately the water is clear and warm and the river bottom is only 5 m down. No crocodiles around, but plenty of freshwater turtles sculling about just above the mud and big shoals of tilapia fish. We crouch on the river bottom back to back, keeping our eyes peeled. Five minutes pass and then – is it? – yes, it is – materialising out of the distant gloom, floats, dances almost, a mighty form. You turn to watch as I nudge you. The creature ignores us as it passes, followed by another and then another. An underwater procession of

The 'mini' hippo – the pigmy hippopotamus.

Lumbering on land, the hippo prances elegantly underwater.

giants. Over 3 m long and weighing up to 3 tonnes or more, the hippos move through the water with the greatest of ease.

Glorious mud

The *hippopotamus* is the largest *even*-toed mammal alive on earth (pigs, camels, deer, giraffes, sheep and cattle also have an even number of toes on their feet, while horses, tapirs and rhinoceroses have an odd number). Its closest relative is the pig. There are two living kinds of hippo – the hippopotamus that inhabits African grasslands, rivers and lakes, and the *pigmy hippo*, a forest dweller found only in a few parts of West Africa. Long ago hippos similar to these modern species lived all over Europe and in some regions of Asia.

The smooth skin of the hippo is thick, but evaporates water up to five times quicker than that of humans. So, during the day, the hippo messes about in water to avoid losing serious quantities of body liquid, and goes to feed on land during the cool of the night.

Hippos feed on grass and other plants for about five to six hours during the night. They leave the water and trundle down 'hippo pathways' that they have made (and marked with piles of dung so they can smell their way if necessary in the darkness) which lead to 'hippo lawns' where they graze. These lawns may be up to 2 km inland or even farther, if there are mud wallows along the way which can be used to refreshen and moisten the skin. 'Mud, mud, glorious mud!' is truly their theme song.

15

A dentist's nightmare – a hippo saying 'Aarh!!'

During the day, therefore, the hippo lazes and dozes in the river. It can stay under water for around five minutes. Its eyes, ears and nostrils are placed on the top of its head, so that it can lounge in the water with just those organs protruding above the surface. Its bulky body in water has a specific gravity of approximately 1 (the same as fresh water), so it can move about easily without any risk of sinking like a rock or bobbing up like a cork. Hippos are surprisingly agile creatures who can swim quite fast. And under water they spring like ballet dancers!

When the hippos have passed us by I tap you on the shoulder and indicate that we should surface. We paddle to the bank where we sit and watch a dozen or so hippos who have hauled out on to the mud. A few birds, oxpeckers and egrets have landed on the backs of the hippos, who are totally unconcerned at being used as convenient platforms for feeding.

Nursery tales

Although they look placid, hippos can be very dangerous. It is particularly risky for people to approach the mud bank or sand-bar nurseries or 'creches' on which young hippos and their mothers are lying. Getting too near solitary old bulls can also bring about a sudden, devastating charge. One snap of those immense jaws can cut a boat, or a man, in two.

Hippo society, like that of elephants, is organised on herd lines led by females. The female hippos command their territory from the central creche. Important breeding males live on surrounding nearby mud banks while young males take up properties farther away. Baby hippos are born either on land or in shallow water, and some births actually occur underwater. As soon as it's born, the baby paddles up to the surface to take its first breath.

Hippo mothers take great care of their babies who suckle their milk either on land or in the water, and often the babies

16

lie on their mother's back when they are in deeper water. Sadly, nearly half of all baby hippos die within the first year of life. But if they survive, they can live for over 30 years, and individuals of 40 or more have been recorded in zoos.

The claim that hippos sweat blood is without foundation, although they *look* sometimes as if blood is oozing out of their skins while they bask in the sunshine.

Get out of the way – fast! Charging hippos can be very dangerous.

However, the red liquid is not blood but rather a coloured sweat-like liquid which is, would you believe, a natural sun-tan oil! It is possible that it also has antiseptic qualities, because hippo wounds – they often get them when squabbling – heal quickly and cleanly even in the dirtiest water.

★ ★ ★ ★ ★

It is time to return to the balloon to be off on the evening breeze.

Late afternoon, and we are floating slowly through the warm air. Below is an expanse of green and gold savannah, broken here and there with outcrops of rock and clusters of grey-green trees. In the distance, smoke-grey, a line of hills shimmers in the haze. We are in Kenya now.

On we drift until, almost directly under our basket, you spot a small herd of zebra grazing in a tight knot and unaware of our presence, for our shadow is still far to the side of them. Then, as you scan the ground with your binoculars, you make a soft hissing noise.

'Quick, David,' you whisper. 'Look. Over there. *Lion!*'

About 150 m downwind from the zebras, a fine lioness is lying crouched behind the ruins of a broken termite mound. She is staring intently in the direction of the zebras. To her right, another lioness is concealed behind rocks. She also is watching the grazing equines.

'The King of Beasts,' I whisper back. 'We're in luck. That pair of females, act-ing in concert as they usually do, are about to launch an attack. Watch! We'll see the classic moves of a hunting cat – more or less the same as those of your pet cat at home when he's stalking a bird.'

Lionesses do most of the hunting that supplies the pride with food, and we settle to watch their standard hunting techni-que. First, having spotted the target, they approach cautiously, taking advantage of any available cover. That's where the ter-mite mound and rocks come in. This is followed by the so-called 'slink run'. Both lionesses leave cover and move swiftly nearer to the zebras, keeping their bodies flattened close to the ground. Each lioness reaches another 'ambush point' – in both cases a low bush. They pause again, for they are now within 30 m of the zebra who, though nervous, are still unaware of their presence. Now the big cats prepare themselves for the final stage. We can see the hind feet making treading move-

The powerful kick of a zebra can often cope with an attacking lion.

'I won't tell you again!' A lioness scolds her cub.

ments as if rehearsing the dash, the tail tips are twitching furiously and the eyes are fixed on the nearest zebra. Suddenly, the attack is launched. One lioness charges out of cover, keeping her body flat to the ground. The other female follows suit. They sprint across the open ground. Both are homing in on the same young zebra. The zebra herd wheels in a cloud of dust. Hoofs fly. The first lioness springs forward, keeping her hind feet on the ground for stability. She aims for a neck bite but . . . wham! The hind hoofs of a zebra stallion catch her in the chest. She's knocked off balance. The second lioness is momentarily confused. The zebras are now in full flight. The attack has failed.

Lions can reach speeds of 55 kmh, but only over short distances – no chance of catching the zebras this time. Because the prey can often outsprint them, only about one in three of such combined hunting forays by lions are successful. This means that the lion cubs will have to wait for their dinner, which can sometimes be serious. Many cubs starve to death during their first year of life.

Lordly but lazy

The lion has been traditionally respected and admired. The Messiah is referred to in the Bible as the lion of the tribe of Judah. In Islam, Ali, the prophet Mohammed's son-in-law was called the Lion of God for his religious zeal and great courage, an attribute shared with King Richard I of England, Richard Lion-heart. The lion was an emblem, too, of the resurrection stemming from an ancient belief that lion cubs are born dead and remain so for three days, after which the father breathes on them and they come alive.

In heraldry, the lion has always been the symbol of sovereignty and power. There are three lions in the arms of England and one red one in those of Scotland.

The lion is one of the commonest heraldic animals.

A crowned lion was King Henry VIII's badge, and a winged lion is the emblem of the City of Venice. Some fountains traditionally have their water issuing from the mouth of a lion. This is a very old custom dating back to the ancient Egyptians who thus symbolised the annual flooding of the Nile which happens when the sun is in the zodiacal 'house' of Leo, the lion.

Lions long ago were one of the most widespread mammals in the world, to be found right across the northern hemisphere. Until about 2,000 years ago they inhabited south-eastern Europe. In the twentieth century they have become extinct in the Near and Middle East, most of Asia and West Africa and in North and South Africa. *Atlas lions,* from the North African mountains, can nowadays only be seen in zoos such as those at Madrid, Spain and Port Lympne, England. There are five subspecies of lion living in the wild today, of which four are regarded as endangered. The *Asiatic or Indian lion* is preserved now only in a reserve in the Gir Forest in Gujarat, India.

Lions rest up in the midday sun.

Lions live in groups called prides composed of four to twelve females and their cubs which are born one to six in a litter. A pride is defended by one or two males and other males live alone or in bachelor prides. Pride territories, the boundaries of which are marked by roaring, urine marking (like domestic cats) and regular patrolling, can extend over as much as 400 sq. km. Sometimes adjacent territories overlap, but the central zone is always kept solely for the use of the 'home' pride. In the wild lions live for about 15 years, though in zoos and safari parks they often reach 20 years of age or more.

Lions have always borne the title 'Lord of the Jungle'. In fact this is nonsense. Firstly, lions generally live in open bush land and grassy savannahs, or even desert areas, not dense jungle. And, formidable big cats though they are, I don't regard them as being as mighty as the bigger, solitary and exceedingly aggressive tiger or the smaller, elusive leopard. Many of the old big game hunters regarded the leopard as the most dangerous of the large cats, and from my experience I'd go along with that.

Do not disturb

Lions, unlike tigers and leopards, usually hunt in pairs or groups, and, as we have seen, they have little stamina for the

Two lionesses and their cubs go out on the prowl.

chase. Occasionally, however, they do become 'man-eaters'. The Tsavo region of Kenya was once famous for its man-eating lions. At the turn of the century, dozens of people working to construct a railway line to the Indian Ocean were killed by several lions, two of which started the slaughter and accounted for most of the victims. When they were eventually shot, they turned out to be large males without manes. Some man-eater lions have been found to be diseased or incapacitated in some way, and they may have turned to human prey as being easy to catch, but many seem to be physically normal.

Nevertheless, the vast majority of lions one might come across in the wild are *not* aggressive towards man, but rather sleepy, retiring animals, except when hunting their normal prey – antelopes and zebra – when harassed or during the mating season. Lions sometimes tackle other animals. There is a report of a battle between two lions and a buffalo that lasted two hours, and in some areas they kill a fair number of giraffes, including adults. They will take on hippopotamus and occasionally young elephants. Adult elephants and rhinoceros can easily cope with lion attacks and are usually successful in protecting their young, provided the latter stay close to them.

★ ★ ★ ★ ★

'Have you ever seen a cross between a lion and a tiger, David?'

'Yes, several. I looked after one, a tigon – father a tiger, mum a lioness – at Belle Vue Zoo, Manchester for donkeys' years.'

'Do they occur in the wild?'

'No, and they never did. Tigons and ligers are always zoo-born, man-made creations.'

HIGH AND MIGHTY

We have sailed through a balmy star-sprinkled night with the radio providing a succession of appropriate musical accompaniments. While the hare in the full moon (look up and you will see him) watched over us, we travelled on a flower-perfumed breeze. You checked our course with the luminous compass while I made a broth of the mushrooms and wild garlic we had picked after hippo-hunting.

Thank goodness you saw the black outline of the rocks looming towards us.

'Collision!' you shout. I strike the gas control lever with all my might. The flames roar in even greater protest. The thud as the basket strikes ground is less than I had feared. Our container lurches violently threatening to spill us both out. Then we swing level again. The air bears us up once more.

'A close shave,' you mutter, pulling yourself up to the basket side and looking over. The lump of unexpected ground is disappearing behind us.

'A mountain top,' I reply; the impact has dislodged my tweed cap and my head feels cold in the icy air. Scanning the maps by torchlight I recognise the peak over which we have just scraped. Time to put down. Soon it will be dawn and the

This is what long necks are for. A male giraffe can reach to the top of the trees.

Daybreak and the giraffes are already browsing.

eastern horizon is already paling. Ten minutes later we are on terra firma in a clearing surrounded by dimly visible acacia trees.

'Look! Something's moving over there and I can hear it. A tree – it's a tree moving!' you gasp. Sure enough a tree does seem to be passing slowly from right to left in front of us, and there is another.

'Where are we, David?' You sound slightly apprehensive.

'Don't worry, those aren't the moving trees that frightened Shakespeare's Macbeth,' I reassure you. 'They're not trees at all. Look again.' The tall 'trunks' can be seen more clearly now.

'*Giraffes!*' you exclaim. 'Moving through the trees and feeding. So this is our next mighty animal. Do they always feed by night?'

'Giraffes dine for over twelve hours every day, mainly in the twilight, at dawn and dusk, but if there is plenty of moonlight, they adore midnight snacks too.'

As the dawn begins to break, the towering animals browsing in front of us begin to gain colour and their features are steadily revealed. The *high* and mighty animals that we are watching were once called camelopards because they were said to be a cross between a camel and a leopard.

Altitude problems

The giraffe is all legs and neck, far and away the tallest animal on earth. But why? What is the point of being apparently so gawky? In fact, the giraffe is not gawky at all. It gallops with surprising grace and speed, and it can defend itself with powerful well aimed kicks of those heavy-hoofed legs against its principal enemy, the lion, and against hyenas, leopards and hunting dogs which sometimes attack baby giraffes. I was once nearly killed by a bull giraffe that swiped at me with a forefoot. Having such great height is an advantage, firstly in enabling the animal to browse on foliage that is out of reach of other herbivorous animals, and secondly in providing a built-in watch-tower-like ability to spot danger far off.

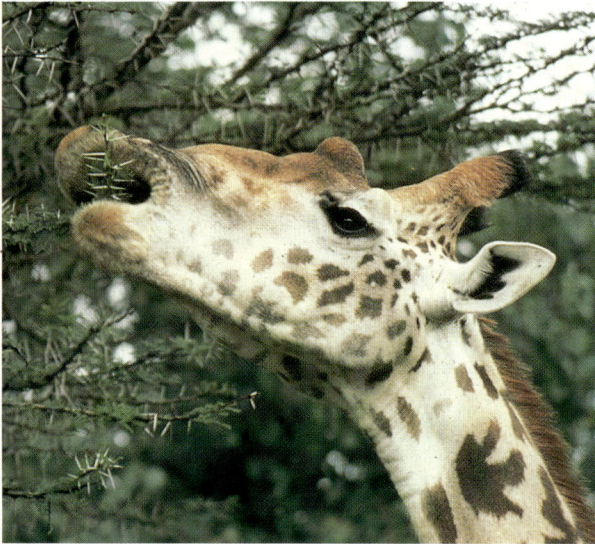

The giraffe's mouth is equipped to deal with prickly leaves and twigs.

On average, big bull giraffes stand 4.5-5.0 m high from the ground to the tips of their peg-like 'horns', but heights of almost 6 m (over 1 m taller than a London double decker bus!) have been recorded. Giraffes have no very long-necked relatives alive today. Their closest living relative is the beautiful, rare and velvet-brown skinned *okapi*, which has a couple of giraffe-like pegs on the head of the male, a longish neck and some light patterning on the legs.

Our own neck, which is only a few centimetres long, has seven bones. So the neck of a giraffe, measuring 2-3 m, must surely contain many more – 50 might be a fair guess. Surprisingly, however, the number is the same – seven. But the giraffe's seven neck bones are very long and heavy.

In order to pump the blood up to the brain of such a tall animal, you might think that the giraffe's heart must be exceptionally big and powerful. In fact it is no bigger than that of a domestic cow. But it does have a curious system of one-way valves in the arteries of the neck to help the blood keep moving up when the animal is standing normally, and to stop blood rushing to the brain when the head is down for drinking. Some years ago I was the first person to measure the blood pressure of a calm, untranquillised, normal giraffe. Oddly, this too isn't much higher than that of a cow.

View from the top

Giraffes are ruminants, cud-chewing animals like cows, but unlike most of these, they are born with horns. The horns, still rather rubbery, lie flat on the head of a newborn baby giraffe, but stand up by the end of the first week of life. They are browsers, loving the leaves and shoots of bushes and trees, particularly those of acacias. It's easy to tell the sex of a giraffe at a distance by observing the way they browse. Male giraffes stretch their necks high up into the trees to eat, while female giraffes arch their necks over to eat foliage lower down. They can easily cope with thorny plants, being equipped with heavily grooved and thickened roofs to their mouths and by producing large quantities of thick saliva that protects the softer parts like the tongue. Giraffes and okapis both have a long, mobile, grey-black tongue which they use to curl round twigs and bunches of leaves which are then plucked off. A giraffe tongue can shoot out as far as 50 cm. The giraffe's front teeth are broad and splayed, with lobed canine (fang) teeth specially for stripping leaves off branches. There are no teeth at the front of the upper jaw – just a hard pad that the lower front teeth bite against when neatly breaking off non-spiky shoots and leaves.

Apart from the lion, the giraffe's principal enemy is man. Some African tribes, particularly in the Sudan, Chad and Ethiopia, have traditionally hunted it, sometimes on horseback, as a source of meat. But the giraffe has also been killed just to take the tail hairs to make bracelets for tourists. The tuft of tail hair serves the giraffe as an efficient fly whisk.

The giraffe has excellent senses of smell, hearing and sight. Its vision is particularly acute. It can detect small movement at a distance of 3 km, and the field of vision is wider than a cinemascope screen, covering almost 270 degrees, thanks

A vulnerable moment for this giraffe as it splays its legs to lick bones on the ground.

largely to the eye's horizontal letterbox-shaped pupil (not round as in the human eye). The animal's height enables it to act as a living watchtower – that is why other creatures such as cattle and wildebeest like to graze near by. Their long-necked friends act as early-warning devices, detecting the approach of predators. Giraffes are at their most vulnerable when they are drinking. To get their head down to the water, they must splay their legs,

and lions like to launch their attacks at such moments. Very sensibly, one or two giraffes always act as sentries with their heads held high when the others are drinking.

Coats of all patterns

Giraffe mothers undergo a pregnancy of about 15 months. The females give birth in giraffe 'maternity hospitals', the same calving grounds that are used year after year. One female may give birth to a dozen babies during her lifetime, although about half of all giraffe calves die during the first six months of life. The mothers often leave groups of calves alone while they go off to feed themselves during the heat of the middle of the day. They know that the lions find it too hot to go out hunting and prefer to lie snoozing at this time, but they are careful to return to guard their offspring when the temperature begins to drop in the late afternoon.

There are generally believed to be nine (although some people say as many as 20) subspecies of giraffe, identifiable by their variations in basic coat pattern. Every individual giraffe has its own unique and

A giraffe calf suckles from its mother.

personal coat pattern that it shares with no other individual. All giraffes live in the savannahs and open woodlands of Africa south of the Sahara Desert. Once they could be found right up to the Mediterranean coastline of North Africa and across to the Atlantic coast in the west. They are not, as a species, endangered, though some subspecies, such as *Rothschild's giraffe* of western Kenya, occur now in only small numbers. Giraffe herds are usually composed of females and youngsters, although there are a few bachelor herds. Bulls tend to live alone.

★ ★ ★ ★ ★

'How fast can a giraffe run?' you ask.

'Up to about 65 kmh, and when they do gallop, the hind legs come forwards and are set down more or less at the same time, outside the forelegs. A thrilling sight.'

'If this is Africa and those are giraffes, what was that mountain top we skimmed?'

'Kilimanjaro – we're in Tanzanian territory.'

'And where do we go next?'

'Nowhere – till we've had breakfast. Watching all those giraffes chomping the foliage has made me quite hungry.'

Some of the different giraffe markings.

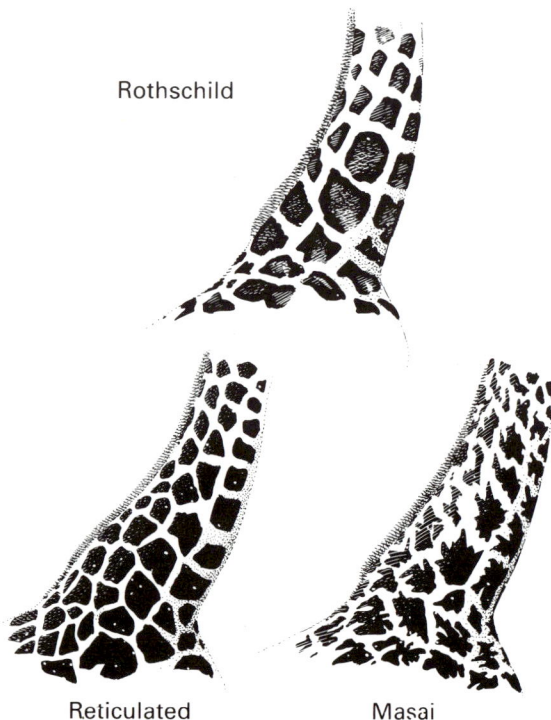

Rothschild

Reticulated   Masai

JUNGLE VICTIM

Get down! Prepare for a rough landing!' I bark out the words as we skim over the trees. There is a sharp crackling sound as the basket touches the topmost branches. Sweating, for it is a furnace-hot, humid afternoon, you grab one of the safety ropes and squat on your haunches. I notice your right-hand fingers are crossed.

KERRASH! Somehow the basket stays more or less upright as we plunge through the tree cover and come to a bumpy halt in a bed of young bamboo. Vine leaves flutter down like confetti and the balloon settles gently over us. There is the smell of sandalwood and damp vegetation. Cicadas thrum steadily and invisibly in the trees. A green snake flicks its tongue at

What on earth is this rhino doing in a hole?

one of our ropes impinging on its resting place, coiled around a branch. Far away, perhaps alarmed by our noisy landfall, monkeys hoot.

There are other noises too, coming from near by. A dull thudding, the heavy crunching of vegetation under foot, husky breathing and the occasional deep grunt. We climb warily out of the basket and I lead the way, pressing apart the bamboo and tall grass.

It's hard going in the dense undergrowth, but I don't want to use the machete I've brought along, until we know what it is that is making the noises.

Beyond a jumble of rotting fallen tree trunks coated in bright green moss, we find ourselves standing in a more open space. To right and left an indistinct trail runs through the trees. Bushes have been

27

broken down, undergrowth trodden into a damp carpet – it is some sort of pathway, but surely not man-made.

'Our next mighty animal is somewhere around,' I say, wiping the streams of stinging sweat from my face. 'Come on, let's turn right and follow its highway.'

'But David, it's quite narrow – what if we come face to face with whatever it is – coming the other way?'

'Say a prayer to St Francis,' I reply, 'but don't worry – it's a strict vegetarian and wouldn't fancy eating you!'

A Sumatran rhino at home in the jungle.

We have walked barely 100 m when I stop. 'Look!' I say. In front of us a large rectangular hole yawns in the pathway. The thudding, crunching, grunting noises are loud now – and they are coming from the hole!

'What on earth is it?' you whisper. Then, 'I know – a giant armadillo digging into the earth – we're in South America!'

'Wrong – we're far away from there. This is the Far East, a land, actually an archipelago, comprising over 3,000 islands and part of what was once the Dutch East Indies.'

'I give up,' you reply, 'but let me *please* look into the hole!' We move slowly forwards and peep over the edge. At the bottom of a 2 m deep pit cut into the earth with vertical sides stands a stocky animal, perhaps 3 m long, that bears two short horns on its snout and is covered all over with coarse reddish hair. A *rhinoceros*. But a very special, very rare rhinoceros. From time to time he rams his muscle into the black earth wall that faces him. He grunts in frustration, paws the ground beneath him and rolls bloodshot eyes.

'How are the mighty fallen! This my young friend is a *Sumatran rhino* – which makes sense, because we are on the island of Sumatra.'

'What's he doing in a hole?'

'The hole is a pit-fall, a trap dug by poachers in one of the pathways made and used regularly by rhinos as they travel through their jungle territory. It would have been camouflaged by the branches and leaves that he's now standing upon.'

'But why? Do they mean to eat him?'

'No – they want just two things – his horns. The stumps of compressed hair, for that is what rhino horn is composed of, which he carries on his nose. In the Orient such rhino horns – it doesn't matter whether they come from Sumatran, *white* or *black rhino* – are greatly prized as being of medicinal value, especially for love potions. Just one good horn can command a price of $30,000!'

'And is it a good medicine?'

'Much of traditional Far Eastern medicine, using all sorts of vegetable and animal products, is effective, and we in the West can learn a lot from it, but we know *for sure* that rhino horn is of no value at all – except to its rightful owner, the rhino!'

'So what are we going to do? Let the poor beast stay in the hole and then be killed just so some fellow can steal its horns?'

'Definitely not – we'll do something.' I take my machete out of its canvas sheath. 'I'll start cutting branches. You carry them to the pit and throw them in. Gradually we'll fill it up so that the rhino's "floor" is raised. It might take us all day –

Mud glorious mud! A Sumatran rhino relishes its wallow.

but if we can do it, eventually he'll be level with the ground and can then escape.'

'Fan-tastic!' you shout. 'Let's get at it!'

By nightfall I am absolutely exhausted. The rhino, stamping about, has trodden down and compacted the bundles of branches you have thrown around him. Now his feet are almost at ground height. Just as you throw in yet another bundle, he suddenly scrambles up the remaining half metre of earth, gives a mighty grunt, and without a glance in our direction, dashes off into the jungle.

'HOORAY!' you bellow – I don't know where you get the energy from. 'He's safe!'

'Thank blooming goodness,' I sigh. 'My arms feel like rubber bands!'

Danger signs

There are five species of rhino alive today. The one in the hole is the smallest, one of the rarest, and, to my mind because of its red hair, the oddest. It is the Sumatran rhino which weighs up to about 800 kg. Only a few hundred such animals, scattered about the jungles, are left alive. The *Javan rhino* is even more endangered, with a world population totalling no more than 50 animals. The black rhino and the white rhino are inhabitants of Africa; and the mightiest of the lot, the *great Indian rhinoceros*, can weigh 2 tonnes and may grow a horn 60 cm in length. It has the most armour-plated look of all the rhinoceros family, and was the one that the great early sixteenth-century artist, Dürer, drew as a wondrous armoured beast. (He, like most Europeans, had never seen a rhinoceros, but only received

A white rhino mother with her calf in South Africa.

descriptions and a sketch from travellers.)

But imagine, 30 million years ago there was a much bigger rhino trundling around Europe and Asia. It was hornless, measured about 11 m long, including its rather long neck, and weighed up to 20 tonnes, a little more than three modern bull elephants! You could have driven a station wagon between its fore and hind legs without the vehicle's roof touching its tummy. That rhino, called *Baluchitherium*, was the largest land mammal that has ever lived. There were many different kinds of rhino all over the earth at one time, with a *woolly rhino* surviving in Europe until about 15,000 years ago.

The fateful horn

The name rhinoceros means literally in Greek 'nose horn'. Rhinos are vegetarians who eat large quantities of plant food. They are very short-sighted, but have an excellent sense of hearing, through those swivelling sound-funnelling ears, and absolutely brilliant powers of smell.

They can reach an age of 40 years or more and tend to live solitary lives except for the females who keep their babies with them until the next one is born. The most friendly of all rhinos is the white rhino – it sometimes forms pairs or bigger groups, up to six or seven, of immature animals. In zoos and safari parks, white rhinos often become as docile and amenable towards their human acquaintances as domestic cattle. The black is much more aggressive. When a rhino charges, it puts its head down and simply goes – guided by sound and smell. It doesn't *look* its target in the eye. Although most of the charges are bluff, simply to frighten the person or animal away, humans who get too close or annoy the animal too much can get into serious trouble.

In nature rhinos don't have any enemies except man, and all because of that horn. As well as for making medicines, men take the horn to make dagger handles which sell for very high prices in Arabia. And there were other uses in days gone by. It was long believed that if a suspect liquid were put into a cup made of rhino horn, it would bubble if it were poisonous.

UNDERWATER ELEPHANT

It is atrocious weather. The unrelenting wind, driving heavy rain before it, has forced us to land. What a desolate place – black, scoured rocks running as far as the eye can see against the mist of rain, patches of brown, wiry grass like mould on the land, and here and there encrustations of moss brittle with ice.

'When the rain stops we'll go to the cliff edge over there and mount a watch on the sea.'

'For a mighty marine monster?' you ask.

'Right. The mightiest animal of its kind.'

'Then it must be – I know – a whale!'

'No. But here's a clue. 'What lives in a rookery?'

'Rooks!'

'Yes, but also something else. Rookery is the name given to the home, on land, of a group of pinnipeds, 'fin-footed' mammals such as seals and sealions.'

'So we're here to see a seal rookery!'

'Exactly – just over the cliff edge is a pebbly beach that happens to be the rookery of a herd of elephants.'

On a cold and windy Patagonian beach, elephant seals are well insulated by their fat.

'Hah!' you guffaw, 'you're teasing me, David – or the crab meat you've just eaten for lunch is off and giving you hallucinations.'

I chuckle and huddle closer to the fire. 'No, they are often called elephants – sea elephants. We are going to watch the giant among seals, the *elephant seal* – a monster that can weigh over 2 tonnes!'

We stagger over the gleaming black rocks to the cliff edge and, swaddled in extra layers of sweaters and waterproofs, look down to the shoreline. The sea is black and boiling, exploding where it rolls against the dark beach into startling white eruptions of foam.

There on the beach are what we have come to see. Dozens of black-brown roly-poly sausages – enormous, plump seals, wobbly and ungainly and bulging with fat as they haul themselves along almost caterpillar-fashion.

'Sea elephants!' you cry against the howling wind. 'But how can they live in such a freezing, unfriendly place? Where are we anyway?'

'This is Tierra del Fuego, the "Land of Fire", at the southern tip of the South American continent. The first Portuguese explorers of the region gave it that name when they saw the many signal fires lit by

A bull elephant seal seems surprisingly proud of his grotesque 'hooter'!

the local Indians as a warning against the "big canoes" of the Europeans. Out there is the south Atlantic, the treacherous seas around Cape Horn and cold water all the way down to Antarctica. Inhospitable to man, but great for elephant seals.'

As we watch, more elephant seals arrive through the breakers and haul out on to the beach, briefly glistening with water.

Suddenly you yell, 'Look, David, a shark – cutting in towards the beach!' I see the triangular dorsal fin slicing through the waves. Black, almost a metre high, the sinister triangle is making straight for a young elephant seal at the water's edge. But it isn't a shark.

'Killer whale!' I shout, and at that moment the black and white body below the fin breaks through the surface. There's a flash of pink, a gleam of ivory teeth, as a great mouth opens. Too late, the elephant seal lumbers for the beach. Half-grounded itself, the killer whale's jaws clamp down on the seal's trunk and a patch of red blooms in the water. The whale arches its spine and backs off into

the next incoming breaker, taking its luckless prey with it. It has all happened in just a few seconds. Stunned, you turn to stare at me. 'Does that often happen?' you ask.

'Quite often. Apart from man, quite recently, the elephant seal has only two natural enemies – the killer whale and the great white shark. And it is virtually defenceless against them.'

Unlikely athletes

Male elephant seals may reach a length of 6 m and females 3 m, with waist measurements of up to 3.5 m. These huge animals are ungainly, almost ridiculously clumsy, on land (quite a number of seal pups are squashed to death by adults as they heave themselves about on the beaches), but don't be deceived. Their bodies are superbly designed and efficient for life in deep, dark, cold water where they spend the majority of their time. Lacking, like all true seals, external ears, and with smooth, rounded bodies, they are streamlined for cutting through the water. They propel themselves by means of the hind flippers (unlike sealions who 'row' through the water with their fore flippers) and keep the front limbs tucked into the body to reduce water resistance or use them as rudders to help steering.

In the sea, therefore, these animals are amazingly agile and athletic. Even chimps and cheetahs do not possess a backbone as flexible as that of an elephant seal, which can bend over *backwards* to form a 35 degree V shape. Beneath the skin is a thick layer of special, semi-liquid, fat (blubber) which is both an insulator against the cold and a store of food.

Elephant seals are superb divers, able to go down to at least 650 m and stay under for half an hour, hunting the fish, squid and crabs on which they feed. To go so deep for so long they conserve oxygen in their bodies by slowing their heart beats and, by shutting down certain blood vessels, divert oxygen-rich blood to essential organs such as brain and heart. They can carry down extra oxygen due to the fact that they have 50 per cent more blood, weight for weight, than a human being, and more of an oxygen-storing chemical called myoglobin in their muscles.

Down in the dark depths of the sea, they locate their prey thanks to large eyes with a pupil that dilates enormously in poor light. Behind the light-sensitive retina of the eye is a 'mirror' of special cells that concentrates any available light, and the lens of the eye is ball-shaped (unlike yours which is an ovoid disc) which enables the seal to focus sharply below the surface. They can also hear well under water, detect pressure changes through their sensitive whiskers and, perhaps, a bit like dolphins, employ an echo-location (sonar) system.

Harems and pups

There are two species of elephant seal, the *Northern elephant seal*, which breeds on the Californian and Mexican coasts, and

Two bull elephant seals do battle in the surf.

A mother elephant seal and her baby on the beach.

the *Southern elephant seal*, whose rookeries are situated in the southern tip of South America, Antarctica, the Falkland Islands and a number of other islands in the southern hemisphere. Like the other true (earless) seals, elephant seals evolved from the primitive weasel family group about 14 million years ago (whereas sealions and the other eared seals branched off from the bear's family tree).

Elephant seal society is organised on a 'harem' system with a group of females, perhaps as many as 50 animals, being mated and protected by a dominant bull. Elephant seal pups on the Californian coast are born, beginning in late December, about one week after their mothers arrive on land. The pup weighs around 30 kg. The mother suckles the infant on a very rich milk for one month, during which time its weight triples. Most pups are weaned by early March and the adults then mate and return to the ocean. The youngsters spend their days on land and practise swimming skills at sea during the night. At the end of March, they also set out to sea and, unless ill or injured, don't return to land for just over a year.

Once, elephant seals were greatly threatened by man who hunted them for their oil. By the beginning of this century the number of Northern elephant seals had been reduced to about 100. Now, thanks to conservation efforts and the end of hunting, this species flourishes once again and may number over 100,000.

★ ★ ★ ★ ★

'What incredible animals!' you say. 'Do you think I can get closer to take some photographs?'

'Sure. I suggest you put on your wetsuit and then go down to the rookery and wriggle across the pebbles on your tummy. You'll look like a small and unimportant black seal – of no interest or threat to anybody. Then you'll get your close-ups.'

LEVIATHAN

'Tierra del Fuego was bad, but this is even worse,' you groan, picking at a crust of ice that has formed on the basket rim. We are both wearing our parkas and woollen gloves, and though our faces glow in the light of the burners, they feel numb with the bitter cold. The balloon is travelling slowly on a level course through thin patches of cloud laced with sleet. When we emerge briefly from a cloud, we can see only grey heaving ocean beneath us.

'Hot Bovril and a bacon sandwich coming up,' I reply, trying to sound cheerful as I fumble with the primus stove. 'We are pretty sure to sight our next mighty animal any time now.'

'So we'll see land soon?'

'Not today, I fear.'

You scowl briefly, but then your red face breaks into a smile. 'So it's another mighty sea animal?'

'Yes. The mightiest beast alive on earth.'

'Then it must be – I know – a *whale*!'

'Correct. It is a whale that can grow as long as 30 m and weigh up to 160 tonnes, including a 3 tonne tongue. How many kinds of whale do you know of?'

'Er – over 40, I think. The *sperm*, the *humpback*, the *fin*, the *sei*, the *pilot*, the *killer*, the *beluga*, the . . .'

'And the greatest of them all?' I interrupt.

'The *blue whale*!'

'Right again. We're on course over the South Atlantic, about 300 km off the island of South Georgia.'

'Ship ahoy! Look, there's a ship down there. I'll see if I can identify its flag – yes, there it is. White with a red disc in the centre. Japanese!'

It is indeed a Japanese vessel. I watch it riding through the rolling sea, black hull, white superstructure stained with rust, funnel belching blue smoke and a bulky mast with a crow's nest look-out at the top.

The impressive form of a humpback whale underwater.

'It's a whaler,' I murmur. 'The thing on the bows is the harpoon gun and its platform. I suspect they're after our mighty beast, too!'

'Whalers!' you gasp. 'But I thought whaling had been stopped.'

'Not completely. Some countries, in particular Japan and Iceland, still take a number of whales each year for so-called scientific research purposes.'

'And do they kill blue whales?'

'They're not supposed to – let's drop down below the cloud level and see where that boat is heading.'

Forty metres above the waves we survey the vast monochrome sheet of the ocean that laps Antarctica. All is grey – sea and sky. The Japanese ship is steaming along directly below us. You spot the whale first. A plume of vapour, the 'blow', ascends as the gigantic animal breaks the surface to exhale. Barely a dozen metres from the whaler's bow we see a silvery grey expanse of skin, a double-nostrilled blow-hole and the shadow of an immense body perhaps 20 m long. It is undoubtedly our quarry – a blue whale – the mightiest animal in the ocean.

On board the whaler there is much activity. The man in the crow's nest is speaking animatedly into a hand-held microphone. Two other men are running down a sort of catwalk to the harpoon platform. One takes his place behind the harpoon gun. We can see him swivelling it.

'He's aiming for the whale!' you exclaim. 'But aren't blue whales protected?'

'They are – but sometimes, disgracefully, the rules are broken. Once it's been killed and processed on board the mother ship, a sort of floating butcher's shop, who's to say it ever was a blue whale, and not, say, a fin or sei whale?'

You growl angrily. 'Can't we do something – can't we . . .? Then, on a sudden impulse, you grab one of the smoke flares we carry for emergencies, pull the tab and at once the dense red smoke begins to billow out. 'What the . . . ?' I gasp. Lean-

Caught in the act! A Japanese whaler prepares to harpoon a blue whale.

A blue whale blows (exhales).

ing over the basket side you hurl the flare down towards the harpooner who is still taking aim with the gun that in a moment will send a lump of explosive-containing steel deep into the body of his prey. Well aimed! The flare lands close to the base of the gun mount and the harpooner is at once enveloped in a choking crimson cloud of smoke.

Meanwhile, gloriously, the blue whale has indeed dived – for the moment at least it is safe, perhaps a kilometre down – and it can stay down for a long, long time.

'Time to go,' I say, turning up the burners. 'We'd better get back into the cloud out of range of that pistol.' Moments later we are high in the cold grey mist, unable to see or be seen.

The biggest ever

The blue whale is the largest animal that has ever lived on this planet. Like all whales and dolphins, however, and although it lives its life completely in the sea, it has evolved from a land animal. It is a baleen whale, a member of the group of whales without teeth which sift their food from the sea water by means of baleen (whalebone) plates, rather like rows of bristles, set in the mouth. Some other whales, such as the sperm and killer, along with all dolphins and porpoises have teeth. Blue whales feed almost exclusively on krill, shrimp-like

A mother killer whale and her calf.

creatures that abound in the oceans, particularly where the water is cold and rich in oxygen.

Blue whales spend the summer of the southern hemisphere feeding close to the edge of the Antarctic ice. Then they migrate north for thousands of kilometres over well-known routes to reach breeding grounds in the Indian Ocean. Where these are exactly we still don't know. As they go the whales communicate with one another by underwater sounds that can travel over 5,000 km and they navigate perhaps by having the ability to sense the earth's magnetic field much in the way that pigeons can. They do not appear to be able to echo-locate (use sonar) like toothed whales and dolphins.

Pregnancy in a female blue whale lasts one year and the single 7 m long calf is suckled on milk far richer than any cow's, for six to seven months. A blue whale can live for as long as 80 years. These warm-blooded, air-breathing mammals were hunted almost to extinction by man. Where once, before commercial whaling began, there had been over 200,000 of them in the Southern Ocean alone, by the late 1970s perhaps only 7,000 blue whales remained in the whole world. Today they are, theoretically, protected from whaling, though pollution of the oceans may pose a serious future threat. Their numbers seem slowly to be increasing, but they are still an endangered species. It would be immensely sad if these mighty, harmless and very beautiful creatures were to disappear for good.

CHEQUERBOARD MONSTER

A wild night of screaming winds that toss the balloon around the sky; we have touched the outer edge of the first of the season's hurricanes. Morning dawns on a troubled ocean, blue-black with ranks of frothy breakers on the march as far as the eye can see. To the west sullen clouds, the storm's rearguard, reach down to the water, and in the east a silvery sun rises through the mist, softly illuminating the sandy shoreline that we can see perhaps 20 km away and 700 m below us. There is little noise now, just the familiar creak of the basket. The burners are off.

While you heat some coffee over the stove, I assemble the scuba gear and the inflatable dinghy.

The whale shark is the biggest and yet the gentlest fish in the sea.

'We'll land on the beach right ahead.' I point towards the coast that bristles beyond the sand with the tallest palm trees, rising to 30 m or more, that we have ever seen.

'And where might we be?' you ask as you hand me a steaming mug. 'The Caribbean?'

'Yes. And that is the island of Cuba, the beach at Varadero, to be precise.'

'Ah! So the diving gear must mean we're after some great sea beast of the warmer oceans!' You grin triumphantly.

'A great sea beast for sure – one of the biggest, gentlest, most mysterious and most beautiful,' I reply.

'Give me a clue.'

'Harmless, very rarely seen by man, attractively spotted and as long, perhaps, as two double decker buses.'

'The great sea serpent!'

'No – but enough of the questions, *amigo*, prepare for landing – and don't forget your waterproof camera. With any luck you'll get a snap of the animal that the Cubans call "chequerboard." '

Before you can ask any more questions I turn away to the control cables and set about commencing our descent. Forty minutes later, with the balloon and its basket securely lashed down, we pull the dinghy across the sand and set out on to the rolling sea. Ten kilometres out we throw overboard a sea anchor, strap on the air tanks, flippers, weight belts, and other equipment, and tumble backwards from the dinghy's side into the water.

Five metres beneath the surface it is a still, blue-green, crystal-clear world peopled by shoals of metallic-gleaming coloured fish that move in synchronised drills. We wait hanging in the water. Then I tap your shoulder and point.

Slowly, out of the infinite blue, a shape emerges. It appears to fill the sea. A submarine? No. This is something *alive*. Silently it approaches and we find ourselves face to face with a monster 20 m in length and weighing perhaps as much as 40 tonnes. We are extraordinarily lucky to come across such a beast for, since it was first identified by scientists about 160 years ago, it has only been seen by human eyes about once every 18 months on average; in total, therefore, a mere 115 times. And yet, you and I are in no danger. This is a benign, harmless animal and although it is the giant of its kind, it doesn't have a single bone in its body!

Looking at the massive face from the front, we get a rather frog-like impression, produced by the broad mouth that runs all the way across the snout. Small eyes are set low at the sides of the head. We paddle back as the creature travels sedately on, and thrill to the attractive appearance of its skin.

Beneath, it is a yellowish-white, but the sides and top are grey-brown decorated with a regular grid-pattern of pale lines and a heavy sprinkling of circular yellow spots. With the lines of the grid being evenly spaced and enclosing the spots, the animal's side does indeed remind us of a game of draughts; now we understand why the Cubans call it the 'chequerboard'.

A docile giant

The animal passing before us is the biggest fish in the world, the very rare and little known *whale shark*. Like all sharks, it is a member of a class of fish regarded by scientists as somewhat more ancient and primitive than 'modern' bony fish such as the cod, stickleback and salmon. Sharks have a skeleton that is built, not of bone, but of cartilage, the stuff that forms the framework of our nose and ear flaps. The whale shark has a more humped back than other sharks. Its dorsal fin is rounded and set well down the back. The tail is huge, and from top to bottom tip generally measures about one-quarter the length of the body.

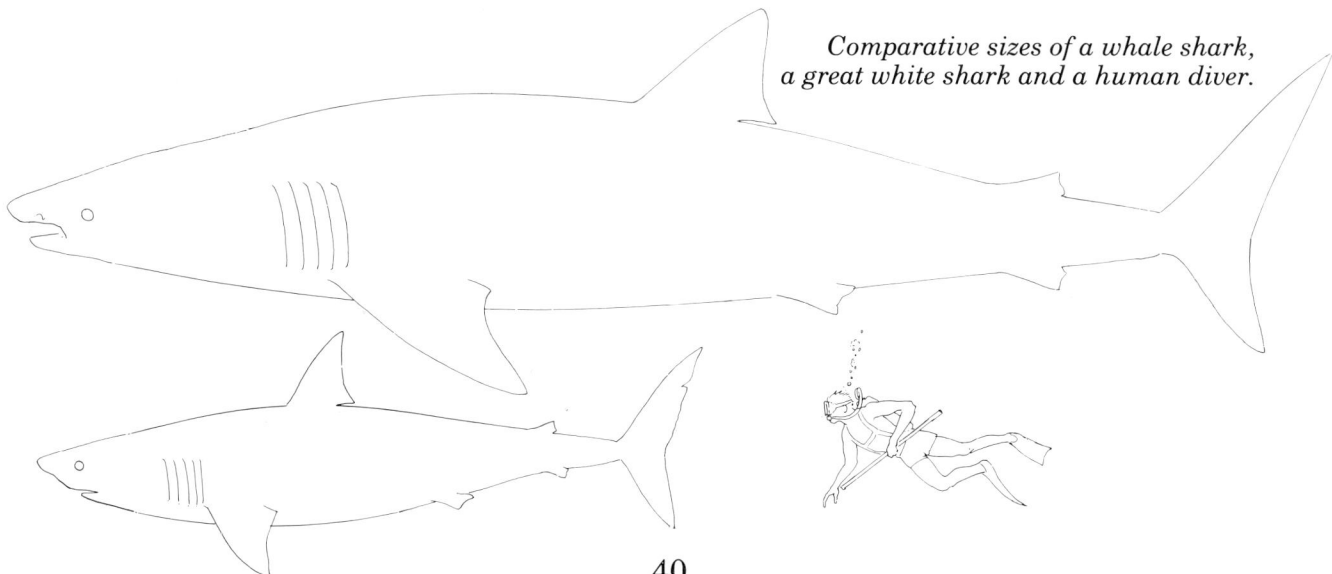

Comparative sizes of a whale shark, a great white shark and a human diver.

So if it's a shark, isn't there a risk of it being a man-eater? After all, the *great white shark* reaches only about 6 m in length and has a fearsome reputation – and this living submarine is over three times as long! No, the whale shark is only interested in feeding on plankton, that teeming broth of the oceans which is composed of microscopic marine life, tiny shrimps and squid, and shoals of little fish. Rather like the baleen or whalebone whales, it gulps down vast mouthfuls of water containing these creatures, clamps shut its jaws that bristle with about 7,000 tiny, spiked teeth, and pumps out the water through its gill-slits. The plankton is sieved out and retained as the water exits by brush-like filters called gill-rakers. It is then swallowed down a rather narrow gullet that has a dog-leg turn in it to prevent the accidental intake of any large items.

Again like the plankton-eating whales, whale sharks need vast quantities of plankton to keep their appetites satisfied. They have normally been seen in a band of tropical waters that extend to about 4,000 km north and south of the equator. Very rarely 'strays' have gone as far north as waters off New York, USA, but the majority of the still few and scattered

A rare photograph – the gigantic whale shark is seldom seen.

sightings of this wonderful fish have been in areas such as the Florida Straits, the Caribbean and the Philippines.

Whale sharks easily hold the size record for fish – the smallest one ever measured was nearly 2 m long, and we have no idea how big the babies are at birth. Very little is known about the life-style of this peaceful leviathan – where does it wander? How long can it live? How big can it grow? Are the babies born alive or in egg-cases?

The whale shark has the amiable temperament of a large dog such as a labrador. Although it never attacks humans, it has upset fishing boats by accidentally brushing against or rising beneath them, for it spends much time basking at the surface. Philippine fishermen dislike it, because of its habit of ruining nets as it blunders on its way.

Now, apparently paying us no attention whatever, our whale shark glides away, its 5 m high tail moving slowly from side to side. Soon it disappears, swallowed by the distant gloom. I wonder when the next sighting of a whale shark will occur. Meanwhile, let's get back to the balloon!

I don't like the look of it! The burners are on full power, but we are losing height. When we flew through a skein of geese just after daybreak, one of them collided violently with the balloon – we must have suffered a rip in the fabric with consequent loss of hot air. No matter, we'll land now.

You are peering through the binoculars at a small collection of wooden houses set in the middle of nowhere. Sagging roofs, doors reeling away from broken hinges, bleached shingles and the rusting remains of a water tower. There is no sign of life in the ghost town. Burners off, make some calculations of wind speed and altitude – with any luck we'll be down on that patch of brown hillside. Must avoid the pillars of rock.

'I've arranged by radio for a friend to meet us with a jeep when we land.'

'But where are we?'

Before I can answer, we bump down and both of us set about the routine task of pulling in the deflating balloon. All around us is rolling grassland, with here and there tall fingers of white rock rising

Echoes of cowboys and Indians – fortunately the buffalo still roam the American plains.

from the plain and some miles away a line of jagged mountains, the colour of rich cream in the sunlight.

'Look!' you shout, pointing, 'What a monster!'

From behind a soaring pillar of weather beaten sandstone 100 m away, a massive brown-black figure moves into view. The large head is held close to the ground as it feeds. The curved horns shine. It is a *buffalo*. Then we see another and another. There must be a dozen or more, all quietly grazing. A trio of beardless chestnut calves interrupt their play to stare in our direction.

Slaughter on the prairie

This is Montana USA, a part of the Great Plains area that encompasses the lands east of the Rocky Mountains from the Canadian border to the mouth of the Arkansas river. Once, enormous herds of these mighty members of the wild cattle family roamed the prairies of this land, and for thousands of years were the chief attraction for the tribesmen who came to live here. Great buffalo-hunting Indian tribes such as the Dakota, Arapaho, Cheyenne, Kiowa, Apache and Comanche, were completely dependent on the

The dangerous African buffalo surrounded by a group of egret admirers.

animals that provided meat for food, horn and bone for implements and skins for leather. Later, with the coming of the horse, firearms and European explorers, the region became peopled largely by roving bands of buffalo hunters. You know the old song, 'Oh give me a home where the buffalo roam, where the deer and the antelope play.'

Where once the buffaloes of the American plains numbered perhaps as many as 50 million, the great herds declined drastically in the nineteenth century as the Wild West was settled by the white men. They hunted the buffalo not only for its commercial value, but also as a means of suppressing the Indians who depended on it for survival. By 1895 only about 800 buffalo were left in the whole of North America and most of them were in Canada. One of the most famous buffalo hunters was William F. Cody, 'Buffalo Bill', who got his name by supplying the men building the Kansas Pacific railway through the wilderness with buffalo meat. He later served in the US 5th Cavalry and killed the Cheyenne chief, Yellow Hand, in single combat. Buffalo Bill died in Denver, Colorado, just over 70 years ago.

It's good to know that conservation programmes, including the setting up of protected reserves such as the Yellowstone National Park, have saved the American buffalo from extinction, and its numbers have risen again to over 50,000. Actually, the famous American buffalo, so often seen stampeding through cowboy films, is more correctly called the *American bison*. It isn't the same as the *water buffalo* of Asia which, domesticated, is to be found also in South America, North Africa and even parts of Europe such as Italy. Nor is it to be confused with the *African buffaloes* which President Theodore Roosevelt, a keen big game hunter, correctly described as 'tough animals, tenacious of life

and among the most dangerous of African game'.

No, the American bison (buffalo) is a different, even more spectacular animal, though it has a close relative, the *European bison* or *wisent*, living in Europe. The latter once roamed over much of Europe, and prehistoric wall paintings of them, some up to 30,000 years old, have been found in caves in Spain, France, Italy and Russia. They too were hunted and by the beginning of this century were reduced to a small herd in the Bialowiecza Forest in Poland and another in the Russian Caucasus. By 1925 they were extinct in the wild. Luckily, re-establishment of the wisent was possible using animals existing in zoos, and today they again roam the wooded lands of Poland and Russia where they are strictly protected.

Dust of battle

The American bison is rather larger and has longer hair on its head and shoulders than the European kind, but otherwise they are very similar in appearance and it may be that they are both subspecies of the bison species. Two kinds of American bison are recognised, the *southern plains bison* and the somewhat darker and larger *wood buffalo* that lives farther north. In 1959 a previously unknown herd of pure wood bison was discovered in Alberta, Canada.

Of all the cattle family, the bison are undoubtedly the mightiest, at least in appearance. Tall and heavy, with a noble, shaggy, bearded head set on powerful forequarters that rise to an impressive hump at the withers, they are imposing animals, particularly when viewed head on. Adult American bison males weigh about 1 tonne and females about 500 kg, but much heavier specimens of as much as 1½ tonnes are on record. The bull bison, nearly twice as big as the female, is a

A buffalo enjoys a dust bath in the afternoon.

The ritual fighting of two American buffalo bulls.

picture of power, an animal whose sole function in life is to challenge and fight other males for the right to mate with cows during the breeding season. Nothing in the world of wildlife is more spectacular than the battling of two bison bulls as they go through their warlike rituals, threatening by swinging their heads up and down, often in unison, bellowing, rolling in the dust and, if one of the pair doesn't give in and move away after all this theatricality, clashing with loud thuds, head against head, vicious horns grinding together and hooves raking the ground. Such contests for the favours of the cows sometimes result in bloody wounds or, less frequently, death. But, as in other species, bison bulls spend more time mock-fighting and trying to intimidate one another, often with great success, than in serious combat. Only about one in seven confrontations end in the gladiators locking horns.

Bison live in groups of 10-20 animals, which merge into much larger herds in the breeding season, July to September.

After a pregnancy of approximately nine months, the cows give birth in April to June. Bison can interbreed with domestic cattle to produce 'cattalos'. In zoos bison can live for up to 25 years.

★ ★ ★ ★ ★

It's time to take a photograph of the buffalo as they slowly move along, grazing, before they disappear from sight. Then we must start inspecting every inch of the balloon fabric to find and patch the leak before we lift off to begin our long journey home. There's at least a week's flying to do before we can shut off the gas burner for the final time. Tell me – which of our ten mighty animals impressed you the most?'

You think for a few minutes, then you say 'I think it was the

. . . .'
(Fill in your own answer here)

A round-the-world journey of adventure

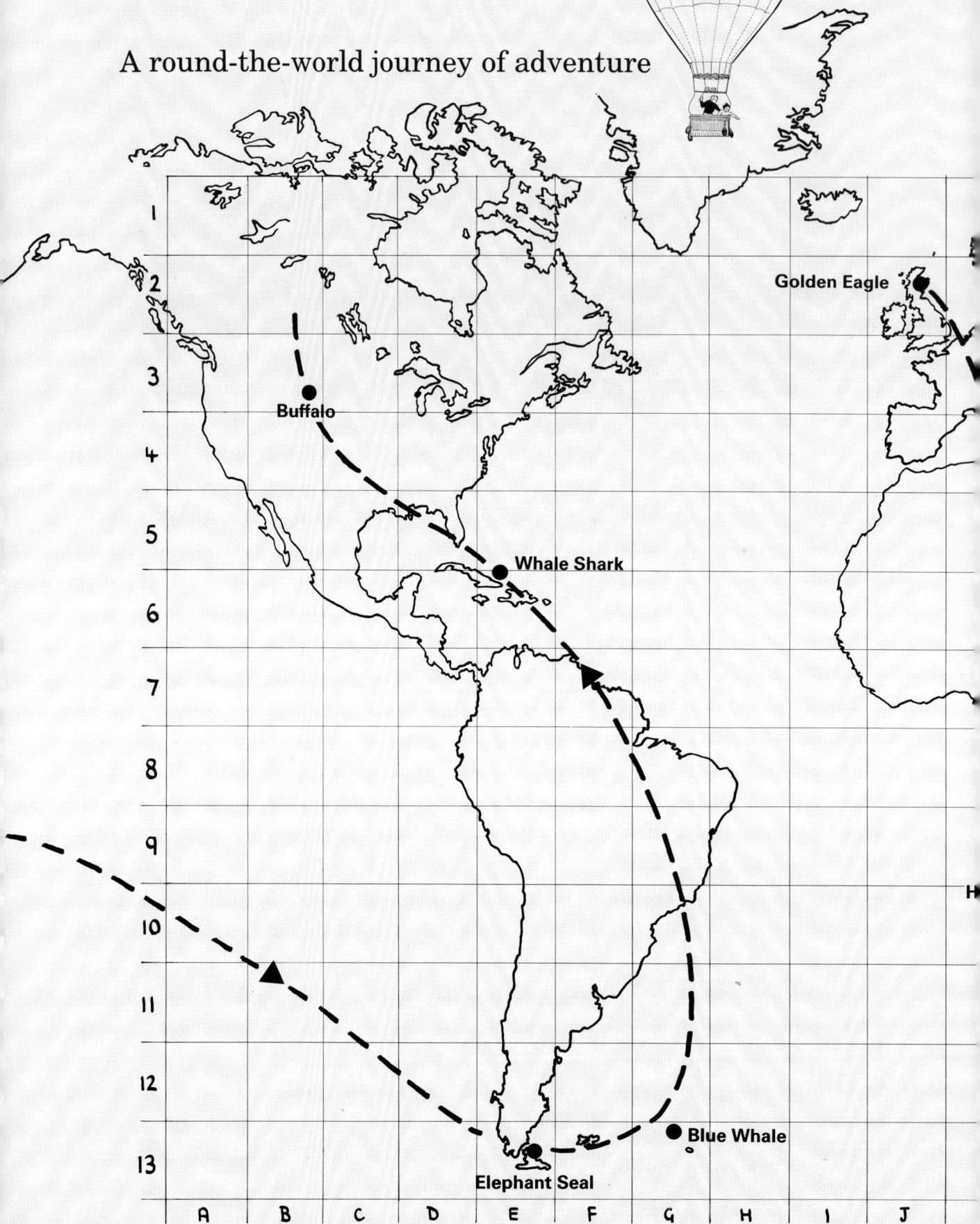

1

2 Golden Eagle

3 ● Buffalo

4

5

6 ● Whale Shark

7

8

9

10

11

12

13 ● Blue Whale

● Elephant Seal

A B C D E F G H I J

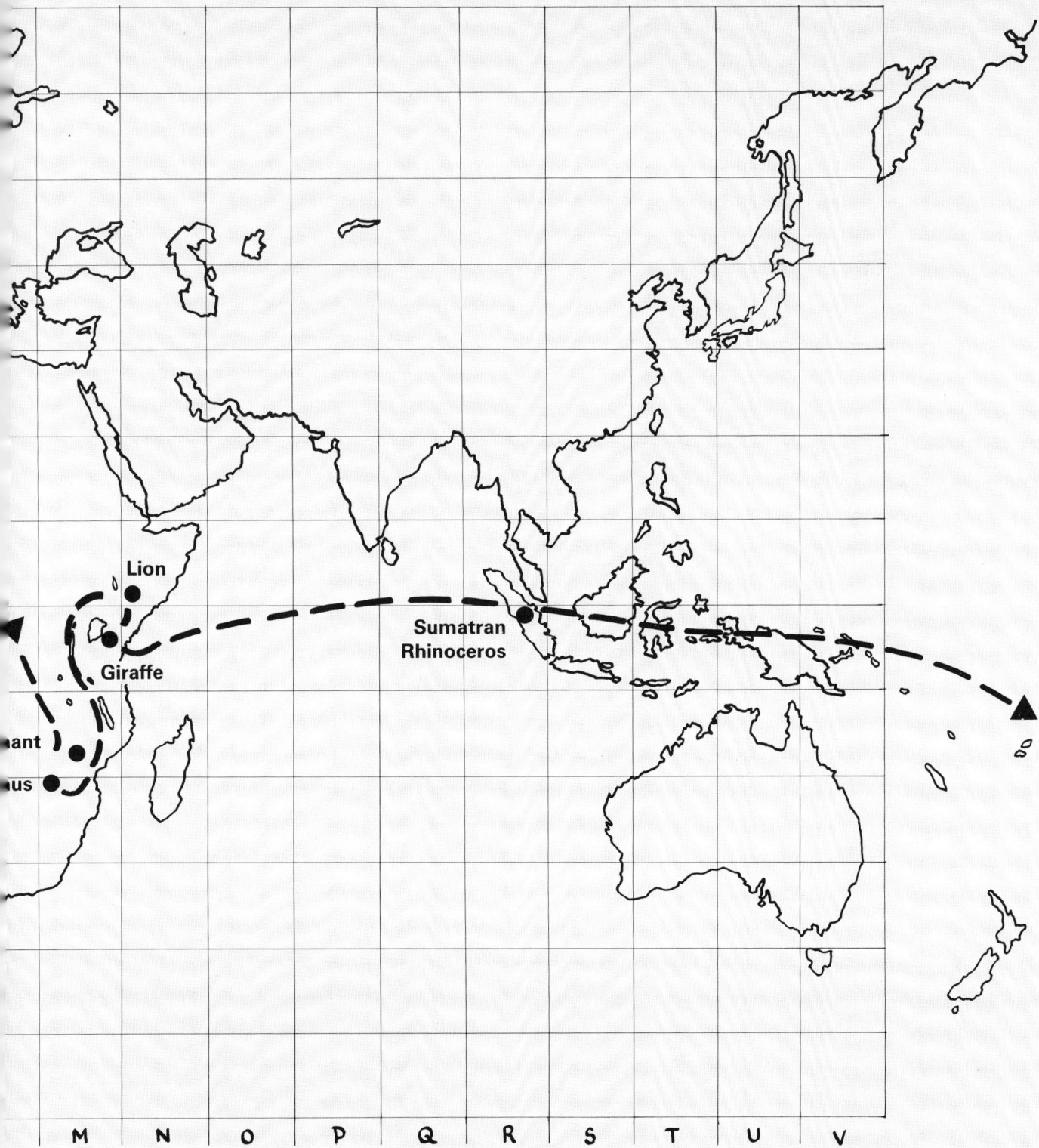